Praise for Allen Klein

"Some of these inspirational quotes are familiar; many are not. All are perfect when you need just the right words to say or—more important—when you need to see the right words yourself."

—Linda Picone,
author of *The Daily Book of Positive Quotations*

"Just when you think you have read everything written on love, Klein puts together a book of 500 quotes ever uttered on the subject of love."

—*New Thought*

"Klein is a successful professional speaker who has already sold half a million inspirational and fun books. This book is a terrific gift item, a great winter pick-me-up, and a valuable reference book for writers and speakers. Consider displaying it prominently where it can generate the maximum number of spontaneous purchases."

—*Retailing Insights*

"Allen Klein will capture your heart.... This eclectic compilation of quotes on every type of love—defining love, falling in love, first love, romantic love, loving couples, motherly love, self-love, physical affection, the overbearing power of love and unconditional love—is perfect for gift-giving or just to keep close for inspiration. Add this one to your bookshelf!"

—Books a la Mode

"Allen Klein has put together a delightful collection of quotes about love. Perhaps it's a piece of work one could be inspired by to write our own words of love. Good material for wedding vows, or whatever one's heart might be compelled to do with such a generous selection of poetic verse and prose. Klein understands that love comes in many forms, suitable for different occasions, relationships and people in our lives, and has grouped the quotes into appropriate categories covering those special events like first love, true love, marriage and even the special love from a mother to a child. These quotes nurture that inherent hope that there's someone out there for everyone. And love nurtures love. These tender heartfelt words will encourage us to share it, feel it, give it away!"

—Laura Friedkin, *San Francisco Book Review*

"Allen Klein takes a subject that seems very overworked and leaky, and manages to pull together a commendable resource for writers and speakers of all stripes. Here you will find quotes from ancient and modern sources; philosophers, actors and writers; and famous and little known creative souls."

—Spirituality and Practice

having
the time *of*
your life

little lessons to live by

Other Viva Editions books by Allen Klein:

Always Look on the Bright Side:
Celebrating Each Day to the Fullest

The Art of Living Joyfully:
How to Be Happier Every Day of the Year

Change Your Life!:
A Little Book of Big Ideas

Inspiration for a Lifetime:
Words of Wisdom, Delight and Possibility

Mom's the Word:
The Wit, Wisdom and Wonder of Motherhood

Words of Love:
Quotations from the Heart

having
the time *of*
your life
little lessons to live by

COMPILED BY
ALLEN KLEIN

FOREWORD BY
LORETTA LAROCHE

V!Va
EDITIONS

Published in the United States by Viva Editions, an imprint of Cleis Press, Inc., 2246 Sixth Street, Berkeley, California 94710.

Printed in the United States.
Cover design: Scott Idleman/Blink
Cover photograph: Sakis Papadopoulos/Getty Images
Text design: Frank Wiedemann

First Edition.
10 9 8 7 6 5 4 3 2 1

Trade paper ISBN: 978-1-936740-70-3
E-book ISBN: 978-1-936740-95-6

Library of Congress Cataloging-in-Publication Data

Having the time of your life : little lessons to live by / compiled by Allen Klein ; foreword by Loretta LaRoche. -- First edition.
     pages cm.
   ISBN 978-1-936740-70-3 (pbk.)
 1. Life--Quotations, maxims, etc. I. Klein, Allen.
 BD431.H3725 2014
 081--dc23
                           2013041138

For my parents,
who first gave me life,
and to all those who
continue to enrich it.

CONTENTS

I have always been interested in enriching and empowering people's lives...in showing them how to lighten up and partake in what I call "juicy living." In other words, helping individuals explore, develop and incorporate the principles of a life that is filled with both energy and enthusiasm.

Through my studies of positive psychology and mind-body sciences, among other modalities, I show people how to look at life in a new way. I remind them that life is not a stress rehearsal and that there is indeed a light at the end of the tunnel.

As a speaker, author, stress management and humor consultant, I have been interested in Allen Klein's work for a long time, because it is similar to what I do. We both teach people how to get a new perspective on life through humor and positive thinking.

In his latest book, *Having the Time of Your Life: Little Lessons to Live By*, Klein and I once again share similar paths in exploring larger concepts, not only related to the perspective that humor can give, but also to what life is and how to fully enjoy it.

In this easy-to-digest, delightful-to-read book, Klein explores the meaning, madness and mirth of life. With the wise and witty words of the rich, the famous and the not-so-famous, Klein divides the book into three interesting categories: "What's Life?," "Why We're Here" and lastly, "How to Enjoy the Journey."

For centuries, great thinkers have pondered what life is. So it is no wonder that the answers in this book are so varied, so funny and so profound. For example, Douglas Adams, author of *The Hitchhiker's Guide to the Galaxy*, says, "The Answer to the Great Question…Life, the Universe and Everything…[is] Forty-two." And, on a deeper level, the French-Algerian philosopher, Albert Camus, reminds us that, "Life is absurd."

Perhaps a bit of absurdity might not be such a bad thing in relationship to trying to figure out not only what life is but also why we are here. Comedian Judy Tenuta jokingly tells us why she is here. She says, "That profound question can be answered in three easy words: TO WORSHIP *ME*." More profoundly, the Dalai Lama believes that, "The very purpose of our life is to seek happiness."

That last quotation from the Dalai Lama fits so well with the final section of the book as it addresses how to enjoy our time on earth. "My advice to you," says author Thornton Wilder, through one of the characters in his play, *The Skin of Our Teeth*, "is not to inquire why or whither, but just enjoy your ice cream while it's on your plate."

I love this book, and its wonderful quips, quotes and anecdotes, because it got me thinking about my life… about why I'm here…and, perhaps most of all, to my way of thinking, how I can get more enjoyment out of my journey. *Having the Time of Your Life* will probably get you thinking about these questions too and perhaps even give you clues on how to enrich, enjoy and enhance your life's journey.

I love what Allen Klein does and I know you will too. So pull up a comfortable chair, get a plate of ice cream and a copy of this thought-provoking book, and get ready for some really juicy reading and juicy living.

Loretta LaRoche
PBS celebrity and author of *Life Is Short, Wear Your Party Pants*

When I was a youngster, *LIFE* magazine was my television. Every Thursday afternoon, it brought the world to my mailbox. It showed me that there were ways of living that were very different from my fifth-floor-walkup Bronx existence. In addition, it showed me the commonalties, struggles and celebrations of all people.

LIFE, the magazine, was also material for a bantering word game I played with my friends. We would repeatedly ask each other:

What's life?
A magazine.
How much does it cost?

Twenty-five cents.
I only have a dime.
That's tough.
What's tough?
Life.
What's life?
A magazine...

LIFE magazine suspended weekly publication many years ago, but the question of "What's life?" still is an intriguing one. Perhaps it is because there are so many answers to such a simple question; perhaps it is because none are right or wrong.

I was hoping that after collecting over 500 quotations that ponder this question, I might have a definitive answer of what life is. The best I could come up with at the end of my research, however, was that life was a magazine I used to read when I was growing up.

Allen Klein
San Francisco

L'Chaim!
(To life!)

J E W I S H   T O A S T

What's a life, anyway?
We're born, we live a little while, we die.
E. B. WHITE

Getting born is like being given a ticket to the theatrical
event called life. It's like going to the theater. Now, all
that ticket will get you, is through the door. It doesn't get
you a good time and it doesn't get you a bad time. You go
in and sit down and you either love the show or you don't.
If you do, terrific, and if you don't—that's show business.
STEWART EMERY

What's life? I really don't know and that's OK. I can live
with that. After all I don't know how my computer works
and I still use that.
RICK SEGEL

The messiness of experience,
that may be what we mean by life.
DANIEL J. BOORSTIN

It is the "just this much" which is the millisecond after
millisecond of awareness and the "just this much" which
contains the enormity of Being found within being, the
sacred Presence that illuminates presence.

STEPHEN LEVINE

Life is a luminous halo, a semi-transparent envelope
surrounding us from the beginning.

VIRGINIA WOOLF

Life is the childhood of our immortality.

JOHANN WOLFGANG VON GOETHE

One life; a little gleam of Time between two Eternities.

THOMAS CARLYLE

Life is a spell so exquisite
that everything conspires
to break it.

Emily Dickinson

The meaning of life lies in the oneness of all creation,
which combines supreme diversity with supreme
interdependence.

YEHUDI MENUHIN

Life is a process of becoming, a combination of states we
have to go through.

ANAÏS NIN

Life is a grindstone. Whether it grinds us down or
polishes us up depends on us.

L. THOMAS HOLDCROFT

Life is a train of moods like a string of beads; and as we
pass through them they prove to be many colored lenses,
which paint the world their own hue, and each shows us
only what lies in its own focus.

RALPH WALDO EMERSON

Life is just a chance to grow a soul.

A. POWELL DAVIES

Life is about authenticity,
recognizing and honoring one's song,
getting in tune with that song and singing it well.

MARGE SCHNEIDER

The meaning of life is quite simple. Sit back, kick the
cruise control into action and enjoy the trip.

TERRY "TUBESTEAK" TRACY

I found out that all the important lessons
in life are contained in the three rules for achieving
a perfect golf swing:
1. Keep your head down.
2. Follow through.
3. Be born with money.

P. J. O'ROURKE

In three words I can sum up everything I've learned
about life: it goes on.

ROBERT FROST

In the book of life,
the answers aren't in the back.

C H A R L E S   S C H U L Z

The meaning of life? It is life itself!

MAREK HALTER

The Answer to the Great Question...of Life, the Universe
and Everything...[is] Forty-two.

DOUGLAS ADAMS

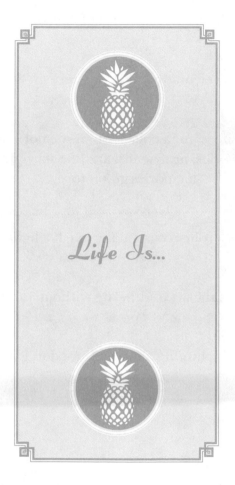

Life Is...

Life is just a bowl of cherries.
LEW BROWN

Life is a celebration of being here on this earth.
MARGIE KLEIN

Life is just a collection of memories…
but memories, my friends, are like starlight because
memories go on forever.
C. W. McCALL

Life is a roller coaster. Try to eat a light lunch.
DAVID A. SCHMALTZ

Life is the art of drawing without an eraser.
JOHN W. GARDNER

Life is painting a picture, not doing a sum.
OLIVER WENDELL HOLMES, JR.

Think, if you will, of your life as an art gallery and of the events in it as paintings that you have made. A week ago or a year ago or just yesterday you began a picture and today it turns up in the gallery that is your life. You stop to look at it. Is it beautiful...or is it ugly...? Whatever it is, see it as a painting in the gallery of your life, and consider that the spirit in which you paint today determines how nice your gallery looks tomorrow.

BRIAN BROWNE WALKER

For a long time it had seemed to me that life was about to begin—real life. But there was always some obstacle in the way, something to be got through first, some unfinished business, time still to be served, a debt to be paid. Then life would begin. At last it dawned on me that these obstacles were my life.

JAMES PATTERSON

Our life is March weather,
savage and serene in
one hour.

RALPH WALDO
EMERSON

Unrest of spirit is a mark of life; one problem after another presents itself and in the solving of them we can find our greatest pleasure.

KARL MENNINGER

Life is to explore, to discover, to delight and be delighted.

NICOLE SCHAPIRO

Life is made up of desires that seem big and vital one minute and little and absurd the next. I guess we get what's best for us in the end.

ALICE CALDWELL RICE

The difference between life and the movies is that a script has to make sense, and life doesn't.

JOSEPH L. MANKIEWICZ

Life is absurd.

ALBERT CAMUS

Of course life is bizarre, the more bizarre it gets, the more interesting it is. The only way to approach it is to make yourself some popcorn and enjoy the show.

ANONYMOUS

Life is full of infinite absurdities, which,
strangely enough, do not even need to appear plausible,
since they are true.

LUIGI PIRANDELLO

Life is just one damned thing after another.

ELBERT HUBBARD

Life is a crowded superhighway with bewildering
cloverleaf exits on which a man is liable to find himself
speeding back in the direction he came.

PETER DE VRIES

Life is a series of steps. Things are done gradually. Every
once in a while there is a giant step, but most of the time
we are taking small, seemingly insignificant steps on the
stairway of life.

RALPH RANSOM

Life is an unfoldment, and the further we travel the more
truth we can comprehend. To understand the things that
are at our door is the best preparation for understanding
those that lie beyond.

HYPATIA

Life is a journey, from birth to death. If you awake to the possibilities of your journey, it will lead you from isolation to connection; from ignorance to knowledge; from pretense to authenticity; and from fear to love.

SUSAN PAGE

Life is indeed a journey. We don't have a map unless we draw one up ourselves, and the road is filled with unknowns. Sometimes there's smooth sailing, sometimes there are potholes, detours, washouts, and never ending sections of major construction. Sometimes we have to speed up, other times we need to slow down, stop, wait, and even back up. But through it all, those of us who truly know how to live are aware that, wherever we may be, it pays to look around and enjoy the scenery.

C. LESLIE CHARLES

I have found life an enjoyable, enchanting, active, and sometimes terrifying experience, and I've enjoyed it completely. A lament in one ear, maybe, but always a song in the other.

SEAN O'CASEY

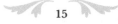

Too often life can seem to be an unpredictable ride between birth and death: we are born without choosing, and die at any time. In between there are many entrances, exits, and detours—some bring great blessings, others great sorrow. Yet we always have some degree of choice—opportunities to fail, or to flourish. Put yourself in the driver's seat as often as possible, and stay awake behind the wheel. Life is a road trip to be experienced to the fullest!

LIAM CUNNINGHAM

Life itself is paradox; both meaningful and meaningless, important and insignificant, a joke and a yoke.

WES "SCOOP" NISKER

Life. It's full of such sadness and sorrow, sometimes I think it's better not to be born at all! But how many people do you meet in a lifetime who were that lucky?

YIDDISH SAYING

A garden is always a series of losses set against a few triumphs, like life itself.

MAY SARTON

Life is tough, but I'm tougher.

ANDY ROONEY

Life is easier than you'd think; all that is necessary is to accept the impossible, do without the indispensable, and bear the intolerable.

KATHLEEN NORRIS

Life is rough for everyone…. Life isn't always fair. Whatever it is that hits the fan, it's never evenly distributed—some always tend to get more of it than others.

ANN LANDERS

When life fits our expectations, we think of it as an opportunity. When it does not, we think the *world* failed us, not our expectations. But that is a mistake, for life will be whatever it wants to be, and not necessarily what we want.

ARNOLD BEISSER

Life is a sum of all your choices.

ALBERT CAMUS

Life works when you choose what you got. Actually what you got is what you chose. To move on, choose.

WERNER ERHARD

Life is an error-making and an error-correcting process,
and nature in marking man's papers will grade him for
wisdom as measured both by survival and by the quality
of life of those who survive.

JONAS SALK

Life is a do-over. Just because you screw up once doesn't
mean you don't get a second chance.

BARRY WISHNER

The art of life lies in a constant readjustment
to our surroundings.

KAKUZO OKAKURA

Life is a game played on us
while we are playing other games.

EVAN ESAR

When I hear somebody sigh,
"Life is hard,"
I am always tempted to ask,
"Compared to what?"

SYDNEY J. HARRIS

Life is a jest, and all things show it;
I thought so once, now I know it.

JOHN GAY

Life is what happens to you
while you are busy making other plans.

JOHN LENNON

Life is something to do when you can't get to sleep.

FRAN LEBOWITZ

You only live once—but if you work it right,
once is enough.

JOE E. LEWIS

The first forty years of life give us the text; the next thirty
supply the commentary on it.

ARTHUR SCHOPENHAUER

Life's a tough proposition, and the first hundred years
are the hardest.

WILSON MIZNER

Life is the biggest bargain. We get it for nothing.

YIDDISH SAYING

That it will never come again is what makes life so sweet.

EMILY DICKINSON

The unfortunate, yet truly exciting thing about your life,
is that there is no core curriculum. The entire place is
an elective…. So if there's any real advice I can give you
it's this. College is something you complete. Life is something you experience.

JON STEWART

Life is my college.
May I graduate well, and earn some honors!

LOUISA MAY ALCOTT

Life Isn't...

Life isn't about finding
yourself. Life is about
creating yourself.

GEORGE BERNARD
SHAW

Your life is not a problem to be solved
but a gift to be opened.
WAYNE MULLER

Life is an enjoyable game to be played—
not a horrible problem to be solved.
KEN KEYES, JR. AND BRUCE BURKAN

Life is not a problem to be solved once; it is a continuing
challenge to be lived day by day. Our quest is not to find
the answer but to find ways of making each individual
day a human experience.
HAROLD S. KUSHNER

Life is not life unless you make mistakes.
JOAN COLLINS

Life is not a problem. If we live, we live; if we die, we die;
if we suffer, we suffer; it appears that we are the problem.
ALAN WATTS

Life isn't a science. We make it up as we go.
AL HIRSCHFELD

Life is a progress, and not a station.

RALPH WALDO EMERSON

Life is not dated merely by years. Events are sometimes
the best calendars.

BENJAMIN DISRAELI

Life is not long, and too much of it must not pass in idle
deliberation how it shall be spent.

SAMUEL JOHNSON

Life isn't all about what you don't have, but yet, what you
do with what you have been given.

ROBERT M. HENSEL

Life is not so bad if you have plenty of luck, a good
physique and not too much imagination.

CHRISTOPHER ISHERWOOD

Life isn't all golf.

TIGER WOODS

Life Is Like...

Life is rather like a tin of sardines—we're all of us
looking for the key.

ALAN BENNETT

Life is like a bagel. It's delicious when it's fresh and warm,
but often it's just hard. The hole in the middle is its great
mystery, and yet it wouldn't be a bagel without it.

ROGER VON OECH

Life is like a sewer.
What you get out of it depends on what you put into it.

TOM LEHRER

Life is like a combination lock; your goal is to find
the right numbers, in the right order, so you can have
anything you want.

BRIAN TRACY

Life is like an onion: You peel
it off one layer at a time, and
sometimes you weep.

CARL SANDBURG

My Mama always said life was like a box of chocolates.
You never know what you're gonna get.

TOM HANKS

Life is like riding a bicycle.
You don't fall off unless you stop pedaling.

ANONYMOUS

Life is like a ten-speed bicycle.
Most of us have gears we never use.

CHARLES SCHULZ

Life is like a dogsled team. If you ain't the lead dog,
the scenery never changes.

LEWIS GRIZZARD

Life is like a library owned by an author. In it are a few
books which he wrote himself, but most of them were
written for him.

HARRY EMERSON FOSDICK

Life is like a mirror. You frown at it, it glares back at you;
you smile at life and it returns the smile.

RALPH RANSOM

Life is like a game of cards.
The hand that is dealt you represents determinism;
the way you play it is free will.

JAWAHARLAL NEHRU

Life is like a B-grade movie. You don't want to leave in
the middle of it, but you don't want to see it again.

TED TURNER

Life is like music, it must be composed by ear, feeling and
instinct, not by rule.

SAMUEL BUTLER

Our lives are like a candle in the wind.

CARL SANDBURG

Life is like an overlong drama through which we sit
being nagged by the vague memories of having read the
reviews.

JOHN UPDIKE

I think of life itself now as a wonderful play that I've written for myself, and so my purpose is to have the utmost fun playing my part.

SHIRLEY MacLAINE

Life is a moderately good play
with a badly written third act.

TRUMAN CAPOTE

Life's like a play: it's not the length,
but the excellence of the acting that matters.

SENECA

Life is like a jigsaw puzzle but you don't have the picture on the front of the box to know what it's supposed to look like. Sometimes, you're not even sure if you have all the pieces.

ROGER VON OECH

Life is like playing the
violin solo in public and
learning the instrument as
one goes on.

S A M U E L   B U T L E R

Life is like a coin. You can spend it any way you wish, but you only spend it once.

LILLIAN DICKSON

Life is like a roll of toilet paper, the closer it gets to the end, the faster it goes.

ANDY ROONEY

Life Is Love

To me life has meaning
because we love.

ELEANOR ROOSEVELT

I believe that the reason of life is for each of us simply to
grow in love.

LEO TOLSTOY

Where there is love there is life.

MAHATMA GANDHI

I have found that if you love life, life will love you back.

ARTHUR RUBINSTEIN

The life and love we create is the life and love we live.

LEO BUSCAGLIA

Love is the ultimate and the highest goal
to which man can aspire....
The salvation of man is through love and in love.

VIKTOR FRANKL

Life is the flower for which love is the honey.

VICTOR HUGO

Life in abundance comes only through great love.

ELBERT HUBBARD

If you give your life as a wholehearted response to love,
then love will wholeheartedly respond to you.

MARIANNE WILLIAMSON

Life is a paradise for those who love many things
with a passion.

LEO BUSCAGLIA

The absolute value of love makes life worthwhile,
and so makes Man's strange and difficult situation
acceptable. Love cannot save life from death; but it can
fulfill life's purpose.

ARNOLD TOYNBEE

You will find as you look back upon your life that the
moments when you have really lived are the moments
when you have done things in the spirit of love.

HENRY DRUMMOND

There is only one happiness in life, to love and be loved.

GEORGE SAND

Life without love is like a tree without blossoms or fruit.

KAHLIL GIBRAN

Keep love in your heart. A life without it is like a sunless garden when the flowers are dead. The consciousness of loving and being loved brings a warmth and richness to life that nothing else can bring.

OSCAR WILDE

Life is so precious. Please, please, let's love one another, live each day, reach out to each other, be kind to each other.

JULIA ROBERTS

If you were all alone in the universe with no one to talk to, no one with which to share the beauty of the stars, to laugh with, to touch, what would be your purpose in life? It is other life, it is love, which gives your life meaning. This is harmony. We must discover the joy of each other, the joy of challenge, the joy of growth.

MITSUGI SAOTOME

Life has taught us that love
does not consist in gazing
at each other but in looking
outward together in the same
direction.

ANTOINE DE SAINT-
EXUPÉRY

Life is short and we have never too much time for
gladdening the hearts of those who are traveling
the dark journey with us. Oh, be swift to love,
make haste to be kind!

HENRI-FRÉDÉRIC AMIEL

The underlying question at the end of our lives always is,
"How well did I love?"

JOHN WELSHONS

The meaning of life is that we love one another.
The purpose of our lives, it seems to me, is to learn
how to do that, so we can create a world where everyone's
in love with everyone all the time.

MARIANNE WILLIAMSON

In our life there is a single color, as on an artist's
palate, which provides the meaning of life and art.
It is the color of love.

MARC CHAGALL

The supreme happiness in life is the conviction
that we are loved.

VICTOR HUGO

One word frees us of all the weight and pain of life:
that word is love.

SOPHOCLES

Love is life.
And if you miss love, you miss life.

LEO BUSCAGLIA

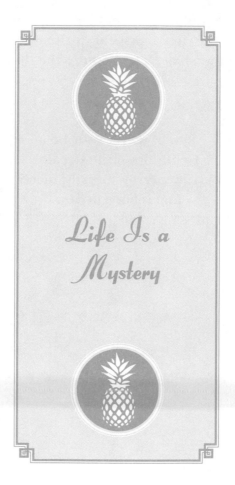

Life Is a
Mystery

Life is a roar of bargain and battle; but in the very heart of it there rises a mystical spiritual tone that gives meaning to the whole. It transmutes the dull details into romance.

OLIVER WENDELL HOLMES, JR.

Row, row, row your boat
Gently down the stream.
Merrily, merrily, merrily, merrily
Life is but a dream.

TRADITIONAL SONG

What if everything is an
illusion and nothing exists?
In that case, I definitely
overpaid for my carpet.

WOODY ALLEN

Life's meaning is a mystery.
BETTY FRIEDAN

Life is about not knowing, having to change, taking the
moment and making the best of it, without knowing
what's going to happen next. Delicious ambiguity!
GILDA RADNER

There's nothing more ironic or strange
or contradictory than life itself.
ROBERT DE NIRO

Life is an end in itself, and the only question
as to whether it is worth living is whether
you have had enough of it.
OLIVER WENDELL HOLMES, JR.

The great business of life is to be, to do,
to do without, and to depart.
JOHN MORLEY

Life is a great and wondrous mystery, and the only thing
we know that we have for sure is what is right here right
now. Don't miss it.

LEO BUSCAGLIA

What is life? An illusion, a shadow, a story. And the
greatest good is little enough: for all life is a dream, and
dreams themselves are only dreams.

PEDRO CALDERON DE LA BARCA

The mystery of existence is the connection between our
faults and our misfortunes.

MADAME DE STAËL

If you want my final opinion on the mystery of life and all
that, I can give it to you in a nutshell. The universe is like
a safe to which there is a combination. But the combination is locked up in the safe.

PETER DE VRIES

Nobody gets to live life backward. Look ahead, that is
where your future lies.

ANN LANDERS

Life can only be understood backwards;
but it must be lived forwards.

SØREN KIERKEGAARD

Living is an art, not a science.
You make it up as you go along.

AL HIRSCHFELD

Life is the art of drawing sufficient conclusions from
insufficient premises.

SAMUEL BUTLER

Life is uncharted territory.
It reveals its story one moment at a time.

LEO BUSCAGLIA

Our life is a faint tracing on
the surface of mystery.

ANNIE DILLARD

Why We're Here

Why are we here? To enjoy the experience of being alive.
Yes, that's it! Quite simple, really.

ED BRODOW

Personally, I think the reason we are here is that it was
too crowded where we were supposed to go.

STEVEN WRIGHT

We are here to give jobs to census takers.

MALCOLM KUSHNER

The very purpose of existence is to reconcile the glowing
opinion we hold of ourselves with the appalling things
that other people think about us.

QUENTIN CRISP

"Why are we here?" That profound question can be
answered in three easy words: TO WORSHIP *ME*.

JUDY TENUTA

Why are we here?
Short answer:
We're here to experience the highest level of joy possible.
Long answer:
We're here to fulfill our purpose. If you know what it is,
you're to enjoy the journey that you've set for yourself. If
your purpose is not crystal clear, then your purpose is to
discover your purpose.

SUSAN SCOTT

A life devoted to things is a dead life, a stump; a God-
shaped life is a flourishing tree.

PROVERBS 11:28

If you want to know why you were placed on this planet,
you must begin with God. You were born *by* his purpose
and *for* his purpose.

RICK WARREN

To know and to serve God, of course, is why we're here.

GARRISON KEILLOR

The secret of man's being is
not only to live but to have
something to live for.

FYODOR DOSTOYEVSKY

One needs something to believe in,
something for which one can have whole-hearted
enthusiasm. One needs to feel that one's life has
meaning, that one is needed in this world.

HANNAH SENESH

Unless you assume a God, the question of life's
purpose is meaningless.

BERTRAND RUSSELL

You were made by God and for God—and until you
understand that, life will never make sense.

RICK WARREN

To achieve a miraculous experience of life,
we must embrace a more spiritual perspective.
Otherwise, we will die one day without ever having
known the real joy of living.

MARIANNE WILLIAMSON

Every man's life is a fairy tale written by God's fingers.

HANS CHRISTIAN ANDERSEN

For everything that lives is holy, life delights in life.

WILLIAM BLAKE

Just to be is a blessing, just to live is holy.

ABRAHAM JOSHUA HESCHEL

Life becomes religious whenever we make it so: when some new light is seen, when some deeper appreciation is felt, when some larger outlook is gained, when some nobler purpose is formed, when some task is well done.

SOPHIA LYON FAHS

An authentic life is the
most personal form of
worship. Everyday life has
become my prayer.

SARAH BAN
BREATHNACH

While we are just a grain of sand in the great flow of
time, we are, each of us, unique and necessary to the
fulfillment of some cosmic plan.

KATHLEEN BREHONY

The goal of life is living in agreement with nature.

ZENO

We are here to fulfill our potential. We are born as seeds.
Either we choose to nurture the seed with the right soil
and the right climate, bloom into a flower and share our
unique beauty with the world, or we die as a rotten seed.
It is our choice.

PRAGITO DOVE

There is no meaning to life except the meaning man
gives to his life by the unfolding of his powers.

ERICH FROMM

Life has no meaning unless one lives it with a will, at least
to the limit of one's will.

PAUL GAUGUIN

No pleasure philosophy,
no sensuality, no place nor power, no
material success can for a moment give such inner
satisfaction as the sense of living for good purposes,
for maintenance of integrity, for the preservation
of self-approval.

MINOT SIMONS

We are here to express our unique version of life, to say,
"This being, this me, is part of Life." Just the way that
pine tree gives off its pine scent and says, "I'm not an oak
tree or a pig. I'm a pine tree; get used to it."

NEIL FIORE

We can discover this meaning in life
in three different ways:
(1) By creating a work or doing a deed;
(2) By experiencing something
or encountering someone; and
(3) By the attitude we take toward unavoidable suffering.

VIKTOR FRANKL

"Why are we here?" is surely the most important question human beings must face…. Our obligation is to confer meaning to life and, in doing so, overcome temptations of passivity and indifference.

ELIE WIESEL

The purpose of life is to live a life of purpose.

ROBERT BYRNE

The purpose of life is to
listen—to yourself, to your
neighbor, to your world
and to God and, when the
time comes, to respond
in as helpful a way as you
can find…from within and
without.

FRED ROGERS

I don't think any of us really *knows* why we're here. But I think we're supposed to *believe* we're here for a purpose.

RAY CHARLES

We're here to hold each other's souls...one laugh, one tear at a time...until we figure out why we are here.

SARANNE ROTHBERG

Why are we here? The question "why" is continually being answered by the omnipresent crows of the world— "Be-CAWS, be-CAWS, be-CAWS."

WES "SCOOP" NISKER

The question is not "Why are we here?" but "How should we live our lives?"

MORTIMER ADLER

Why are we here? Why aren't we more here? Why leave our life half consumed from day to day? The problem is we are not here we are only dreaming we are any where at all. And it could be such a startling brilliant dream but it ain't, just a dull interpretation of lost worlds.

STEPHEN LEVINE

I don't believe life has a purpose. Life is a lot of
protoplasm with an urge to reproduce
and continue in being.

JOSEPH CAMPBELL

My good friend Jacques Monod spoke often of the
randomness of the cosmos. He believed everything in
existence occurred by pure chance with the possible
exception of his breakfast, which he felt certain was made
by his housekeeper.

WOODY ALLEN

Maybe we are part of someone's experiment to determine whether we can figure out why we are here, and our
confusion, like that of rats in a maze, is the whole point.

WES "SCOOP" NISKER

I believe our Heavenly Father invented man because He
was disappointed in the monkey.

MARK TWAIN

We are here and it is now. Further than that all human
knowledge is moonshine.

H. L. MENCKEN

Life is nothing more than the happiness you get out of it.

JEAN ANOUILH

I believe that the very purpose of our life
is to seek happiness.

DALAI LAMA

The purpose of life, after all, is to live it, to taste
experience to the utmost, to reach out eagerly and
without fear for newer and richer experiences.

ELEANOR ROOSEVELT

The purpose of life is to live it as fully as possible, and to
be grateful every day for the privilege of sharing.

LEONARD BERNSTEIN

The reason we are here is to ask "Why are we here?" and
have the question go unanswered.

MARC KRAVITZ

There ain't no answer. There ain't gonna be any answer.
There never has been an answer. That's the answer.

GERTRUDE STEIN

I was in New York's Metropolitan Museum of Art when an old woman comes up to me and says "Excuse me young man. Can you tell me what time it is?" I look at my watch and say, "It's exactly two o'clock." She tells me that she had a two o'clock appointment with friends, but they aren't here. Then, she continues on, without a comma or period, that she was rarely late for appointments, knew nothing about primitive art, worked at the Bronx Botanical Gardens. I'm day-dreaming, looking at her, five-foot-two-inches, neatly dressed in a blue suit with a matching pillbox hat. In her white-gloved hand, she is carrying a handbag. Politely trying to get away, I hear her say "That's the secret of life." I know I've missed something so I ask her "What's the secret of life?" And she says "Sneakers are the secret of life." I have no idea what she is talking about but as I look down more carefully I see that accompanying her Easter ensemble, she is wearing sneakers. I know I've missed something so I ask her "How are sneakers the secret of life?" And she repeats, "I wear these sneakers because they are only comfortable when you keep moving. That's the secret of life; you gotta keep moving."

CARL HAMMERSCHLAG

How is it possible to find meaning in a finite world, given
my waist and shirt size?

WOODY ALLEN

Can you imagine what would happen if the mystery of
life and our existence was solved? If all the answers, plots,
characters, goals, destinies, procedures, and processes
were revealed? All of a sudden God and creation would
become boring.

MYLES R. BERG

Who knows why we're here? No one knows. You can say
you do, but you can't. All you can say is what I said. It ain't
over 'til it's over. And that's all.

YOGI BERRA

I am here for lunch.

FRANK CHIN

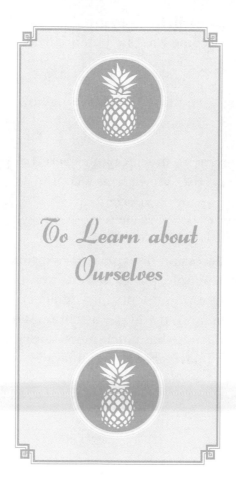

To Learn about
Ourselves

Man's main task in life is to give birth to himself, to
become what he potentially is.

ERICH FROMM

As long as you live, keep learning how to live.

SENECA

Never become so much of an expert that you stop
gaining expertise. View life as a continuous learning
experience.

DENIS WAITLEY

Life is a succession of experiences sprinkled with
emotions, people, places, adventures, triumphs,
wonders, disappointments, puzzlements, injustices,
loves, losses, and, if you pay attention, lessons that
make the journey that much more savory and easily
navigable along the way.

ERIKA LENKERT

Each person has his or her own purpose and distinct
path, unique and separate from anyone else's. As
you travel your life path, you will be presented with
numerous lessons that you will need to learn in order to
fulfill that purpose. The lessons you are presented with
are specific to you; learning these lessons is the key to
discovering and fulfilling the meaning and relevance of
your own life.

CHÉRIE CARTER-SCOTT

Life gives us not only our genetic packages,
but also a certain style of character, a style of being,
and our gifts uniquely equip us for certain callings,
through which we both grow into our fullest humanity,
and nourish the world around us.

DAVIDSON LOEHR

First of all, life is a journey…every experience is here
to teach you more fully how to be who you really are.

OPRAH WINFREY

Your only obligation in any lifetime is
to be true to yourself.

RICHARD BACH

The enjoyment of the journey comes by learning
to love myself despite my imperfections, limitations
and vulnerabilities.

MARGE SCHNEIDER

Why are we here? To take "Life 101," a curriculum of life
experience through which we can awaken into the
fullness of our being.

RAM DASS

If we search outside ourselves for the meaning of life, we
tend never to find it. But if we center ourselves and look
for meaning *in* life, it's always waiting for us, right here in
the present moment.

BO LOZOFF

The purpose of life, then, is
to lovingly accept ourselves
and each other, without bias
or prejudice, as we learn to
unveil the divine spark within.

BARBARA BRENNAN

I find that when we really love and accept and approve of ourselves exactly as we are, then everything in life works.

LOUISE HAY

Even if the patterns of my life do not conform to my preconceived vision of how I wished or expected things to be, every moment is a learning opportunity. Every moment is sacred. Every moment offers me a unique challenge. And, no matter how much I may protest, every moment is perfect for me at that time.

JEFFREY MISHLOVE

There are no mistakes, no coincidences. All events are blessings given to us to learn from.

ELISABETH KÜBLER-ROSS

When you ask yourself, "Why am I here?" or "Why is this happening to me?" or "What's it all about?" turn to your spiritual primer. Ask yourself, "What is the lesson?"

CHÉRIE CARTER-SCOTT

Life is a succession of lessons which must be lived to be understood.

RALPH WALDO EMERSON

There comes a time when it lies within [a man's] grasp to shape the clay of his life into the sort of thing he wishes to be. Only the weak blame parents, their race, their times, lack of good fortune, or the quirks of fate.

LOUIS L'AMOUR

Living on this earth is such a rich experience. If we stand back from our lives, sounds, sights, and smells, experiences profane and sublime whirl and blend deliciously into a tapestry of lush colors and multiple textures. If we stand farther back and look in, we can see how our life is a shining thread in a larger tapestry, the fabric of all life.

ERIN EVERETT

The meaning of our life is to experience the divinity of ourselves and of all creatures.

WILLIGIS JÄGER

Life is a test, a school where we come to learn and grow in our spiritual understanding and personal development, a school designed for each of us to reach our own unique destiny. Each of us is here to learn, to grow, to master the challenges that we face, and to expand our capacity for love and compassion. Taking life on with courage, trusting that we are meant to learn from every experience in life is why we are here.

JUDY TATELBAUM

Life is a test. It is only a test. Had this been a real life you would have been instructed where to go and what to do.

POSTER SAYING

Here is a test to find whether your mission on earth is finished; if you're alive, it isn't.

RICHARD BACH

Don't go through life, grow through life.

ERIC BUTTERWORTH

To Serve
Others

I believe we are all here to be bright torches that light
one another's way.

BERNIE S. SIEGEL

Each of us has a spark of life inside us, and our highest
endeavor ought to be to set off that spark in one another.

KENNY AUSUBEL

We're not primarily put on this earth to see through one
another, but to see one another through.

PETER DE VRIES

Only a life lived for others is a
life worthwhile.

ALBERT EINSTEIN

My only real answer to "What's life?" is: "If you know my
life you will know my answer. And if I know your life, I'll
know yours."

DAVID KUNDTZ

Life is an exuberant gift from a Divine power
that can't resist sharing the miraculous experience
of existence with others.

JESSICA PRENTICE

Most of all, it's about using your life to touch or poison
other people's hearts in such a way that could have never
occurred alone. Only you choose the way those hearts are
affected, and those choices are what life's all about.

ANONYMOUS

Life is partly what we make it, and partly what it is made
by the friends we choose.

TEHYI HSIEH

For me life is speaking for those who no longer can.

NICOLE SCHAPIRO

What's life?
The short answer: a cereal.
The long answer: an opportunity for us all to grow
physically, spiritually and emotionally within ourselves
and through the interactions with others.

RON CULBERSON

The journey is not about helping ourselves, but about
helping others. We do best when we use our own skills to
make a positive difference in the lives of others. When
we do this, we bring enjoyment, hope and fulfillment to
others, but we also find that we enjoy the journey more
than we ever could have imagined.

DAVE LIEBER

The more you focus on making others happy,
the less self-focused you'll become and
the more cheerful you'll be.

SOL GORDON AND HAROLD BRECHER

If you have made another person on this earth smile,
your life has been worthwhile.

MARY CHRISTELLE MACALUSO

To enjoy the journey is to leap into people's lives. To
enjoy the journey is to give until the stretch is a
sacrifice…. The question always is: what is it in life that
will pull you out of your seat to be brave, risk, and serve?

JANIE JASIN

What is the use of living, if it be not to strive for noble
causes and to make this muddled world a better place for
those who will live in it after we are gone? How else can we
put ourselves in harmonious relation with the great veri-
ties and consolations of the infinite and the eternal? And
I avow my faith that we are marching towards better days.

WINSTON CHURCHILL

When it's all over, it's not who you were.
It's whether you made a difference.

BOB DOLE

It's loving and giving that make life worth living.

POPULAR SAYING

If I can stop one heart from breaking,
I shall not live in vain.
If I can ease one life the aching,
Or cool one pain,
Or help one fainting robin
Unto his nest again,
I shall not live in vain.

EMILY DICKINSON

Each of us was placed here for a special purpose. I
believe that it is each person's responsibility to determine
what he or she can do to make the world a better place—
and then go out and do it.

ROSS PEROT

Whatever the reasons for our being here,
surely one of them must be to give us the opportunity
to do something, at least in some small way,
to make the world a better place.

CLEVELAND AMORY

Service is what life is all about.

MARIAN WRIGHT EDELMAN

When people are serving, life is no longer meaningless.

JOHN W. GARDNER

A man who becomes conscious of the responsibility he bears toward a human being who affectionately waits for him, or to an unfinished work, will never be able to throw away his life. He knows the "why" for his existence, and will be able to bear almost any "how."

VIKTOR FRANKL

I think the purpose of life is to be useful, to be responsible, to be honorable, to be compassionate. It is, after all, to matter: to count, to stand for something, to have made some difference that you lived at all.

LEO ROSTEN

I've learned that people will
forget what you said, people
will forget what you did, but
people will never forget how
you made them feel.

MAYA ANGELOU

The life I touch for good or ill will touch another life,
and that in turn another, until who knows where the
trembling stops or in what far place my touch will be felt.

FREDERICK BUECHNER

I am of the opinion that my life belongs to the
community, and as long as I live it is my privilege
to do for it whatever I can.

GEORGE BERNARD SHAW

We don't accomplish anything in this world alone…and
whatever happens is the result of the whole tapestry of
one's life and all the weavings of individual threads from
one to another that creates something.

SANDRA DAY O'CONNOR

We are here on earth to do good for others.
What the others are here for, I don't know.

W. H. AUDEN

The purpose of life…is to be useful, to be honorable, to
be compassionate, to have it make some difference that
you have lived and lived well.

RALPH WALDO EMERSON

One's life has value so long as one attributes value
to the life of others, by means of love, friendship,
indignation, and compassion.

SIMONE DE BEAUVOIR

Life's meaning amounts to how we actually
manage to live it with others.

ROBERT COLES

We are here to add what we can to life,
not to get what we can from life.

WILLIAM OSLER

The influence of each human being on others
in this life is a kind of immortality.

JOHN QUINCY ADAMS

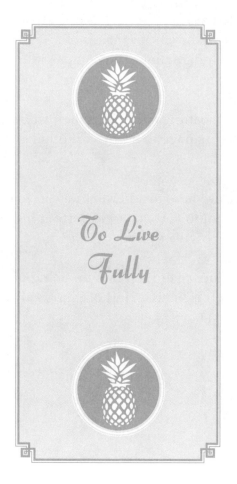

To Live
Fully

Life itself is the proper binge.

JULIA CHILD

Life loves the liver of it.

MAYA ANGELOU

Live life to the fullest.

ERNEST HEMINGWAY

A man who dares to waste one hour of life
has not discovered the value of life.

CHARLES DARWIN

May you live all the days of your life.

JONATHAN SWIFT

Life is too deep for words,
so don't try to describe it, just live it.

C. S. LEWIS

We are misled from early childhood to think that life is
something you get through. Life is something to be in.

DUSTIN HOFFMAN

Life leaps like a geyser for
those willing to drill through
the rock of inertia.

ALEXIS CARREL

Life is a festival only to the wise.

RALPH WALDO EMERSON

To say yes, you have to sweat and roll up your sleeves
and plunge both hands into life up to the elbows.

JEAN ANOUILH

Life is a dance. Squeeze the juice out of each
moment and we find our authentic self. There is no
greater benediction.

PRAGITO DOVE

"What came over you to make you dance like that?"
"What could I do, boss? My joy was choking me. I had to
find some outlet. And what sort of outlet? Words? Pff!"

NIKOS KAZANTZAKIS

Life is about dancing together or dancing apart;
but just keep dancing.

NICOLE SCHAPIRO

Dancing…is no mere translation or abstraction from life;
it is life itself.

HAVELOCK ELLIS

We should consider every day lost on which
we have not danced at least once.

FRIEDRICH NIETZSCHE

On with the dance, let joy be unconfined,
is my motto; whether there's any dance to dance
or any joy to unconfine.

MARK TWAIN

Try as much as possible to be wholly alive, with all your
might, and when you laugh, laugh like hell, and when you
get angry, get good and angry. Try to be alive. You will be
dead soon enough.

WILLIAM SAROYAN

Too many people are thinking of security instead
of opportunity. They seem to be more afraid
of life than death.

JAMES F. BYRNES

The tragedy of life is not so much what men suffer, but
rather what they miss.

THOMAS CARLYLE

Look, I really don't want to wax philosophic, but I will say
that if you're alive, you got to flap your arms and legs, you
got to jump around a lot, you got to make a lot of noise
because life is the very opposite of death. And therefore,
as I see it, if you're quiet, you're not living. You've got to
be noisy, or at least your thoughts should be noisy and
colorful and lively.

M EL B R O O K S

Life is a great big canvas, and you should throw
all the paint you can on it.

D A N N Y K A Y E

Life should be lived so vividly and so intensely that
thoughts of another life, or of a longer life,
are not necessary.

M A R J O R Y S T O N E M A N D O U G L A S

The person who has lived the most is not the one with
the most years, but the one with the richest experiences.

J E A N - J A C Q U E S R O U S S E A U

We live in deeds, not years; in thoughts, not breaths;
in feelings, not in figures on a dial.
We should count time by heart-throbs. He most lives
Who thinks most, feels the noblest, acts the best.

PHILIP JAMES BAILEY

Life is not measured by the number of breaths we take,
but by the moments that take our breath away.

ANONYMOUS

I would urge you to be as imprudent as you dare.
BE BOLD, BE BOLD, BE BOLD.

SUSAN SONTAG

Step outside of your comfort zone often, express your truth with others, proactively love and be loved, explore, rejoice in everyday wonders, don't take things personally; fully feel, express, and release pain and anger; seek and express joy; don't let fear stop you from pursuing your dreams; be "game" for life, dismiss unnecessary drama, make a point of doing what you love, pamper yourself and others, play and laugh often, decide that true richness is a fulfilling life rather than a bank account figure, find and learn from life's "lessons," roll with the punches, and when all else fails, when angry: beat the s**t out of pillows until your arms go limp with fatigue and when sad, turn up your favorite song full blast and dance like crazy. It does the trick every time.

ERIKA LENKERT

Find something that moves you or pisses you off, and do something about it. Put yourself out there. Be brave. Be bold. Take action. You have a voice. Speak up, especially when something tries to keep you silent. Take a stand for what's right. Raise a ruckus and make a change. You may not always be popular, but you'll be part of something larger and bigger and greater than yourself. Besides, making history is extremely cool.

SAMUEL L. JACKSON

Only when we are no longer afraid do we begin to live.

DOROTHY THOMPSON

Do not be too timid and squeamish about your actions.
All life is an experiment.

RALPH WALDO EMERSON

Life is a promise; fulfill it.

MOTHER TERESA

I could not, at any age, be content to take my place by the
fireside and simply look on. Life was meant to be lived.
Curiosity must be kept alive. One must never, for
whatever reason, turn his back on life.

ELEANOR ROOSEVELT

Life is best experienced with a sense of awe, wonder,
and discovery. Go about life with a child's curiosity. The
universe is more spectacular than you can imagine.

TOM GREGORY

People say that what we're all seeking is a meaning for life…. I think what we're seeking is an experience of being alive, so that our life experiences on the purely physical plane will have resonances within our innermost being and reality, so that we actually feel the rapture of being alive.

JOSEPH CAMPBELL

Late on the third day, at the very moment when, at sunset, we were making our way through a herd of hippopotamuses, there flashed upon my mind, unforeseen and unsought, the phrase, "Reverence for Life."

ALBERT SCHWEITZER

Develop an interest in life as you see it; the people, things, literature, music—the world is so rich, simply throbbing with rich treasures, beautiful souls and interesting people. Forget yourself.

HENRY MILLER

The longer I live, the more beautiful life becomes.

FRANK LLOYD WRIGHT

Life begets life. Energy creates energy. It is by spending
oneself that one becomes rich.

SARAH BERNHARDT

Is not life a hundred times too short for us
to bore ourselves?

FRIEDRICH NIETZSCHE

There was never yet an
uninteresting life. Such a
thing is an impossibility.
Inside of the dullest exterior
there is a drama, a comedy,
and a tragedy.

MARK TWAIN

To live is so startling it leaves little time for anything else.

EMILY DICKINSON

There are only two ways to live your life. One is as though nothing is a miracle. The other is as though everything is a miracle.

ALBERT EINSTEIN

What we call the secret of happiness is no more a secret than our willingness to choose life.

LEO BUSCAGLIA

When making your choice in life, do not neglect to live.

SAMUEL JOHNSON

Man is born to live, not to prepare for life.

BORIS PASTERNAK

People do not live nowadays— they get about ten percent out of life.

ISADORA DUNCAN

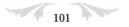

Live all you can; it's a mistake not to. It doesn't so much matter what you do in particular, so long as you have your life. If you haven't had that, what have you had?

HENRY JAMES

Dost thou love life? Then do not squander time, for that's the stuff life is made of.

BENJAMIN FRANKLIN

Life is ours to be spent, not to be saved.

D. H. LAWRENCE

I decided long ago never to look at the right hand of the menu or the price tag of clothes— otherwise I would starve, naked.

HELEN HAYES

What good are vitamins? Eat four lobsters, eat a pound of caviar—live!

ARTHUR RUBINSTEIN

Life is short. Eat dessert first.

POPULAR SAYING

Life is too short to do anything for oneself
that one can pay others to do for one.

W. SOMERSET MAUGHAM

Life is too short to stuff a mushroom.

SHIRLEY CONRAN

If we really want to live we must have the courage to
recognize that life is ultimately very short and that
everything we do counts. When it is the evening of our
life we will hopefully have a chance to look back and say:
"It was worthwhile because I have really lived."

ELISABETH KÜBLER-ROSS

To enjoy life more fully you must keep reminding
yourself that life is too short to waste on unhappiness.

SOL GORDON AND HAROLD BRECHER

I like living. I have sometimes been wildly,
despairingly, acutely miserable, racked with sorrow,
but through it all I still know quite certainly that just
to be alive is a grand thing.

AGATHA CHRISTIE

Live as if you were to die tomorrow....
Learn as if you were to live forever.

MAHATMA GANDHI

Remember, life is not what happens to you but what you
make of what happens to you. Everyone dies, but not
everyone fully lives. Too many people are having "near-
life experiences."

ANONYMOUS

People's whole lives do pass in front of their eyes before
they die. The process is called "living."

TERRY PRATCHETT

Life is either a daring adventure or nothing.

HELEN KELLER

It matters not how long we live, but how.

PHILIP JAMES BAILEY

It is good to have an end to journey toward; but it is the
journey that matters, in the end.

URSULA K. LE GUIN

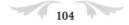

If my doctor told me I had
only six minutes to live, I
wouldn't brood. I'd type a
little faster.

ISAAC ASIMOV

Live your life and forget your age.
NORMAN VINCENT PEALE

Our care should not be to have lived long
as to have lived enough.
SENECA

It is better to wear out than to rust out.
RICHARD CUMBERLAND

There is no cure for birth and death,
save to enjoy the interval.
GEORGE SANTAYANA

We were not born to survive. Only to live.
W. S. MERWIN

And in the end, it's not the years in your life that count.
It's the life in your years.
ABRAHAM LINCOLN

You can't do anything about the length of your life, but
you can do something about its width and depth.
EVAN ESAR

I don't want to get to the end of my life and find that
I lived just the length of it. I want to have lived the width
of it as well.

DIANE ACKERMAN

Let us so live that when we come to die even the
undertaker will be sorry.

MARK TWAIN

When you were born, you cried and the world rejoiced;
live your life so that when you die, the world cries and
you rejoice.

CHEROKEE SAYING

How to Enjoy
the Journey

Life is to be enjoyed, not just endured.

GORDON B. HINCKLEY

The greatest act of revolution in contemporary life, is to
come to every day with joy.

CARL HAMMERSCHLAG

When you think you've had all the joy you can tolerate,
you've only reached *your* limit, not joy's. Use that moment
to expand your limit. Don't just increase joy by a little.
Double it. Then, double that. Discover that your capacity
to know joy is as limitless as joy itself.

JOHN-ROGER AND PETER McWILLIAMS

Write it on your heart that every day
is the best day in the year.

RALPH WALDO EMERSON

This is the day the Lord has made.
We will rejoice and be glad in it.

PSALMS 118:24

One of the greatest gifts God has given you is the ability to enjoy pleasure…. He wants you to enjoy life, not just endure it.

RICK WARREN

There is too much emphasis on success and failure, and too little on how a person grows as he works. Enjoy the journey, enjoy every moment, and quit worrying about winning and losing.

MATT BIONDI

All animals, except man, know that the principle
business of life is to enjoy it.

SAMUEL BUTLER

If man could only realize that God created men and
animals to enjoy life, not to destroy it, then man most
probably would be a lot happier.

ISAAC BASHEVIS SINGER

Think of your life as if it were a banquet where you would
behave graciously. When dishes are passed to you, extend
your hand and help yourself to a moderate portion.
If a dish should pass you by, enjoy what is already on
your plate. Or if the dish hasn't been passed to you yet,
patiently wait your turn.

EPICTETUS

My advice to you is not to inquire why or whither, but just enjoy your ice cream while it's on your plate—that's my philosophy.

THORNTON WILDER

There are two things to aim at in life: first to get what you want; and, after that, to enjoy it. Only the wisest of mankind achieve the second.

LOGAN PEARSALL SMITH

I finally figured out the only reason
to be alive is to enjoy it.

RITA MAE BROWN

No man is a failure who is enjoying life.

WILLIAM FEATHER

Enjoy life...the alternative is just so unpleasant....
And stop spending so damn much time analyzing,
whining, kvetching.

SUSAN ROANE

Sing more, complain less.

MATT WEINSTEIN AND LUKE BARBER

Don't slow down for yellow lights, buy cereal with a prize
in the box and always control the remote.

MALCOLM KUSHNER

How can we enjoy the journey?
Short answer: sex, drugs, and rock and roll.
Long answer: by using our gifts and skills in a way
that enhances our own life and adds value
to the lives of others.

RON CULBERSON

Find your bliss, pursue what gives you the most
joy in life, support others to do the same, and make
absolutely certain that your life is not harming any
other person or diminishing the freedom of others
to find and pursue their bliss!

SUSAN PAGE

Have interesting failures…. If you need to have a
personal crisis have it now. Don't wait until midlife,
when it will take longer to resolve….
Don't pity yourselves. Lighten up. Seek people
with a sense of humor. Avoid humorless people—
and do not marry one, for God's sake.

GARRISON KEILLOR

The most wasted of all days is that
on which one has not laughed.

NICOLAS DE CHAMFORT

Life is duck soup…and we are the laughingstock.

SWAMI BEYONDANANDA

Life is a tragedy when seen in
close-up, but a comedy
in long-shot.

CHARLIE CHAPLIN

I have always felt that laughter in the face of reality is probably the finest sound there is and will last until the day when the game is called on account of darkness. In this world, a good time to laugh is any time you can.

LINDA ELLERBEE

We are all here for a spell;
get all the good laughs you can.

WILL ROGERS

Always laugh when you can. It is cheap medicine.

LORD BYRON

That man is a success who has lived well,
laughed often, and loved much.

ROBERT LOUIS STEVENSON

True life lies in laughter, love, and work.

ELBERT HUBBARD

Take time to laugh, cry, and be silent.

PRAGITO DOVE

Laugh it off, laugh it off; it's all part of life's rich pageant.
ARTHUR MARSHALL

I call no man wise until he has made the progress from the wisdom of knowledge to the wisdom of foolishness, and become a laughing philosopher, feeling first life's tragedy and then life's comedy.
LIN YUTANG

Life is a mannafestival, the FUNdamentalist scriptures tell us, and it is our mannafest destiny to manifest manna—and to have fun doing it.
SWAMI BEYONDANANDA

The comic spirit masquerades in all things we say and do. We are each a clown and do not need to put on a white face.
JAMES HILLMAN

The secret of life is play. Play and humor are what refine and enhance our joy.
SUSAN SCOTT

Without an active spirit of play your rocket never gets off
the ground. It fizzles and sputters around in the driveway.

CY EBERHART

Every good journey needs a GPS system. Not a global
positioning satellite but a Gotta Play Some system.
Whatever pressures, demands, expectations,
and heartache we have in our lives,
we need to take time out to play.

SCOTT FRIEDMAN

Do not take life too seriously.
You will never get out of it alive.

ELBERT HUBBARD

Life is too short for men to take it seriously.

GEORGE BERNARD SHAW

The one serious conviction that a man should have is that
nothing should be taken too seriously.

NICHOLAS MURRAY BUTLER

Not a shred exists in favor of the idea that life is serious.

BRENDAN GILL

Don't worry, be happy.
MEHER BABA

He who would travel happily must travel light.
ANTOINE DE SAINT-EXUPÉRY

Loosen up:
It's not so important to be serious as it is to be serous
about the important things. The monkey wears an
expression of seriousness that would do credit to any
great scholar. But the monkey is serious because he
itches. What can you take less seriously?
ROGER VON OECH

The highest form of bliss is living
with a certain degree of folly.
ERASMUS

As soon as you have made a thought, laugh at it.
LAO TZU

How we can enjoy the journey?
By connecting with others no matter how brief the
encounter. When two spirits join in the moment, there is
no pain, fear, or anger—only joy, hope, and love!

JACKI KWAN

We enjoy the journey by emphasizing those qualities
in our lives which acknowledge, or demonstrate, our
essential Oneness with ALL forms…. We are most happy
when we feel most connected…. Conversely, we are most
unhappy when we feel disconnected, isolated and alone.

JOHN WELSHONS

How can we enjoy the journey? By WO-HE-LO. This is a
short way to say Work Health and Love. This is the motto
of the Camp Fire Girls.

ELIZABETH PROVIDENTY

Happiness doesn't require much, just an easy attitude
'bout yourself and life, a few interests, some people who
love you, and doing things that make you feel good.

BOBBY MCFERRIN

You never find happiness until you stop looking for it.

CHUANG TZU

Belong…to yourself, to the earth, to others. Above all, engage in "radical self-acceptance."

SANDRA SCHRIFT

The first and great commandment is, don't let them scare you.

ELMER DAVIS

Life has two rules:
number one, never quit;
number two, always remember rule number one.

DUKE ELLINGTON

Living is a form of not being sure, not knowing what next or how…. The artist never entirely knows. We guess. We may be wrong, but we take leap after leap in the dark.

AGNES DE MILLE

Don't be afraid to take a big step if one is indicated. You can't cross a chasm in two small jumps.

DAVID LLOYD GEORGE

Nothing in life is to be feared.
It is only to be understood.

MARIE CURIE

How we can enjoy the journey?
Accomplish, create, celebrate, and do the things you
really want to do. Then after you have done it all, then
tell your critics to go to Hell because they are only jealous
that you did it all and they didn't.

RICK SEGEL

The greatest pleasure in life is doing
what people say you cannot do.

WALTER BAGEHOT

Run from anyone who tells you he knows the truth,
anyone who touts a party line,
anyone who says he has *the* answer.

CRAIG WILSON

Accept no one's definition of your life,
but define yourself.

HARVEY FIERSTEIN

In the first third, until about twenty-five, have fun. In the second third, from about twenty-five to fifty, get married, have kids. In the third third, from about fifty to seventy-five, trim your sails to match your finances. In the fourth third, from seventy-five plus, you're on your own. Just don't kick dust in our eyes!

GORDON BURGETT

If you get gloomy, just take an hour off and sit and think how much better this world is than hell. Of course, it won't cheer you up if you expect to go there.

DON MARQUIS

The highest wisdom is continual cheerfulness: such a state, like the region above the moon, is always clear and serene.

MICHEL DE MONTAIGNE

He that is of a merry heart hath a continual feast.

PROVERBS 15:15

Cheer up. Life isn't everything.

MIKE NICHOLS

Alter Your
Attitude

Alter your life by altering your attitudes.

WILLIAM JAMES

What is life but what a man is thinking of all day?

RALPH WALDO EMERSON

The moment we awaken in the morning we can
determine the mood of the day, just as a sailor sets his
sails and, regardless of the wind direction,
establishes the course which his ship will take.

LIONEL A. WHISTON

Some folks go through life pleased that the glass is
half full. Others spend a lifetime lamenting that it's
half empty. The truth is: There is a glass with a certain
volume of liquid in it. From there, it's up to you!

JAMES S. VUOCOLO

It's not the load that breaks you down,
it's the way you carry it.

LENA HORNE

Things themselves don't hurt or hinder us. Nor do other
people. How we view these things is another matter.
It is our attitudes and reactions that give us trouble.

EPICTETUS

The art of life isn't controlling what happens,
which is impossible; it's using what happens.

GLORIA STEINEM

The principle of life is that life responds by
corresponding; your life becomes the thing you have
decided it shall be.

RAYMOND CHARLES BARKER

It's a funny thing about life; if you refuse to accept
anything but the best, you very often get it.

W. SOMERSET MAUGHAM

Most of the shadows of this life are caused
by standing in one's own sunshine.

RALPH WALDO EMERSON

Be not afraid of life. Believe that life is worth living, and
your belief will help create that fact.

WILLIAM JAMES

That life is worth living is the most necessary of
assumptions, and were it not assumed,
the most impossible of conclusions.

GEORGE SANTAYANA

How we spend our days is, of course,
how we spend our lives.

ANNIE DILLARD

Whatever is at the center of our life will be the source of
our security, guidance, wisdom, and power.

STEPHEN COVEY

What we are today comes
from our thoughts of
yesterday, and our present
thoughts build our life of
tomorrow: our life is the
creation of our mind.

BUDDHA

Our life is what our thoughts make it.

MARCUS AURELIUS

A great way to enjoy the journey more is to
mindfully focus on the positive side of everything
every step of the way.

SUSAN SCOTT

We all have unwanted thoughts pop into our head from
time to time. But we also have the ongoing opportunity
to choose the thoughts we give precedence to. And the
more attention we give this process, the more control we
have over creating our dream life. We know that good
thoughts create a good life. Ain't it great!

RANDY GAGE

If one thinks that one is happy,
that is enough to be happy.

MADAME DE LA FAYETTE

The secret of life is not to do what you like
but to like what you do.

ANONYMOUS

Learn to wish that everything
should come to pass exactly
as it does.

The art of living is always to make a good thing
out of a bad thing.

E. F. SCHUMACHER

Life is ten percent what happens to me and ninety
percent how I react to it.

CHARLES R. SWINDOLL

It is not the events in our lives that do us in, but the
choices we make about how we come to them, that brings
us joy on the journey.

CARL HAMMERSCHLAG

The important thing in life is not to have a good hand
but to play it well.

LOUIS N. FORTIN

We will often find compensation if we think more of what
life has given us and less about what life has taken away.

WILLIAM BARCLAY

The art of living is the highest calling of all. If we start seeing our life as a work of art-in-progress, we will find that our attitude toward our life will change.

ALEXANDRA STODDARD

There are really only two ways to approach life—as victim or as gallant fighter.

MERLE SHAIN

The art of life is to know how to enjoy a little and to endure very much.

WILLIAM HAZLITT

It's better to light a candle
than to curse the darkness.

C H I N E S E   P R O V E R B

However mean your life is, meet it and live it; do not shun
it and call it hard names. It is not so bad as you are. It
looks poorest when you are richest. The faultfinder will
find faults even in Paradise. Love your life, poor as it is.
You may perhaps have some pleasant, thrilling, glorious
hours, even in a poorhouse.

HENRY DAVID THOREAU

It is not that there is no evil, accidents, deformity,
pettiness, hatred. It's that there is a broader view. Evil
exists in the part. Perfection exists in the whole. Discord
is seeing near-sightedly. And I can choose this broader
view—not that I always should—but I always can.

HUGH PRATHER

Life doesn't require that we be the best—
only that we try our best.

H. JACKSON BROWN, JR.

"I have done my best."
That is about all the philosophy of living one needs.

LIN YUTANG

Be in the
Moment

Life can be found only in the present moment.
The past is gone, the future is not yet here, and if we do
not go back to ourselves in the present moment,
we cannot be in touch with life.

THICH NHAT HANH

Life is made up of years that mean nothing
and moments that mean it all.

C. P. SNOW

Life is a series of seconds; a series of events; a series of
opportunities; and a series of life-giving moments. As we
live fully each moment, we breathe a fullness not only
into our own life, but into the lives of all we touch and
into the very universe itself.

ANNE BRYAN SMOLLIN

Life isn't a matter of milestones, but of moments.

ROSE FITZGERALD KENNEDY

The happiness of life is made up of minute fractions—
the little, soon-forgotten charities of a kiss or smile,
a kind look, or heartfelt compliment.

SAMUEL TAYLOR COLERIDGE

This—this was what made
life: a moment of quiet, the
water falling in the fountain,
the girl's voice…a moment of
captured beauty. He who is
truly wise will never permit
such moments to escape.

LOUIS L'AMOUR

Live today, forget the past.

GREEK PROVERB

Look at life through the windshield,
not the rear-view mirror.

BYRD BAGGETT

The art of living…is neither careless drifting on the one
hand nor fearful clinging to the past on the other. It
consists in being sensitive to each moment, in regarding
it as utterly new and unique, in having the mind open
and wholly receptive.

ALAN WATTS

As we may miss the joy of life by dwelling on the past, so
we miss the possibilities of the present if we expect life's
best days to be in the future. The good days are *now*.

LIONEL A. WHISTON

Live now, believe me, wait not till tomorrow;
gather the roses of life today.

PIERRE DE RONSARD

We're here to feel the joy of life pulsing in us—now.

JOYCE CAROL OATES

We cannot put off living until we are ready. The most
salient characteristic of life is its urgency, "here and now"
without any possible postponement. Life is fired at us
point-blank.

JOSÉ ORTEGA Y GASSET

Before, I always lived in anticipation…that it was all a
preparation for something else, something "greater,"
more "genuine." But that feeling has dropped away from
me completely. I live here and now, this minute, this day,
to the full, and life is worth living.

ETTY HILLESUM

One day at a time—this is
enough. Do not look back and
grieve over the past, for it is
gone; and do not be troubled
about the future, for it has not
yet come. Live in the present,
and make it so beautiful that
it will be worth remembering.

IDA SCOTT TAYLOR

When you stop comparing what is right here and now
with what you wish were, you can begin to enjoy what is.

CHERI HUBER

The aim of life is to live, and to live means to be aware,
joyously, drunkenly, serenely, divinely aware.

HENRY MILLER

We can enjoy this journey by consciously slowing
ourselves down to live the moment in front of us. We find
energy, joy, humor and grace in that moment. We need
to let go of yesterdays and not be planning tomorrows but
truly savor each present moment.

ANNE BRYAN SMOLLIN

Be intent upon the perfection of the present day.

WILLIAM LAW

I am alive today through the grace of a higher being.
Every day is extra.

JOHN KERRY

Life, we learn too late, is in the living, in the tissue of every day and hour.

STEPHEN LEACOCK

I have learned to live each day as it comes, and not to borrow trouble by dreading tomorrow.

DOROTHY DIX

One must never lose time in vainly regretting the past nor in complaining about the changes which cause us discomfort, for change is the very essence of life.

ANATOLE FRANCE

Life is all memory, except for the one present moment that goes by you so quickly you hardly catch it going.

TENNESSEE WILLIAMS

Life is but a day at most.

ROBERT BURNS

The golden moments in the stream of life rush past us, and we see nothing but sand; the angels come to visit us, and we only know them when they are gone.

GEORGE ELIOT

Learn lessons and live in the moment knowing you are mortal. And when in doubt ask: "What would Lassie do?"

BERNIE S. SIEGEL

You don't get to choose how you're going to die. Or when. You can only decide how you're going to live. Now.

JOAN BAEZ

Look to this Day!
For it is Life, the very Life of Life.

KALIDASA

Keep It
Simple

Expect nothing,
live frugally on surprise.

ALICE WALKER

If my heart can become pure and simple like
that of a child, I think there probably can be no
greater happiness than this.

KITARO NISHIDA

When I look back over the years, what stands out to me
isn't the movies or the games of chess or checkers that I
played with my daughter, it's the short trips we took here
and there, what we said, and how we felt or the songs we
listened to during those brief rides. Enjoy the little jour-
neys; make them the rides your life.

JEFF DAVIDSON

Each small task of everyday life is part of the total
harmony of the universe.

THERESA OF LISIEUX

Life is denied by lack of attention, whether it be to
cleaning windows or trying to write a masterpiece.

NADIA BOULANGER

The meaning of life is to see.

HUI-NÊNG, CHINESE SAGE

The whole of life lies in the verb *seeing*.

PIERRE TEILHARD DE CHARDIN

Look. This is your world! You can't not look.
There is no other world.
This is your world; it is your feast. You inherited this; you
inherited these eyeballs; you inherited this world of color.
Look at the greatness of the whole thing. Look! Don't
hesitate—look! Open your eyes. Don't blink, and look,
look—look further.

CHÔGYAM TRUNGPA

To be alive, to be able to see, to walk…it's all a miracle.

ARTHUR RUBINSTEIN

Life is a great bundle of little things.

OLIVER WENDELL HOLMES, JR.

One awakens, one rises, one dresses,
and one goes forth; one returns, one dines,
one sups, one retires, and one sleeps.

PIERRE-ANTOINE-AUGUSTIN DE PIIS

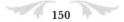

The best things in life are nearest: breath in your nostrils, light in your eyes, flowers at your feet, duties at your hand, the path of right just before you. Then do not grasp at the stars, but do life's plain, common work as it comes, certain that daily duties and daily bread are the sweetest things in life.

ROBERT LOUIS STEVENSON

I'm not going to have a better day, a more magical moment, than the first time I heard my daughter giggle.

SEAN PENN

Life is a child playing around your feet, a tool you hold firmly in your grip, a bench you sit down upon in the evening, in your garden.

JEAN ANOUILH

Ah, the smell of flowers.
I've just put flowers in a vase.
The meaning of life is the
flowers in a vase.

HELEN CALDICOTT

Just living is not enough...one must have sunshine,
freedom, and a little flower.

HANS CHRISTIAN ANDERSEN

If we could see the miracle of a single flower clearly,
our whole life would change.

JACK KORNFIELD

We've all had moments when the heart swells and
we feel wordlessly connected to a larger source of
loving-kindness and compassion: the times when we
surrender to the majesty of a sunset, the caress of a
breeze, the laughter of a child, the eyes of a loved one,
and we know that life is complete just as it is.

JOAN BORYSENKO

What is life? It is the flash of a firefly in the night.
It is the breath of a buffalo in the wintertime.
It is the little shadow which runs across the grass
and loses itself in the sunset.

CROWFOOT

Be glad of life because it gives you the chance to love and
to work and to play and to look up at the stars.

HENRY VAN DYKE

Life moves pretty fast. If you don't stop and look around
once in a while, you could miss it.

MATTHEW BRODERICK

We always have enough to be happy if we are enjoying what
we do have—and not worrying about what we don't have.

KEN KEYES, JR.

I finally understand what life is about;
it is about losing everything…
so every morning we must celebrate what we have.

ISABELLE ALLENDE

Often people attempt to live their lives backwards; they
try to have more things, or more money, in order to do
more of what they want, so they will be happier. The way
it actually works is the reverse. You must first be who you
really are, then do what you need to do, in order to have
what you want.

MARGARET YOUNG

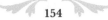

Good friends, good books,
and a sleepy conscience: this
is the ideal life.

MARK TWAIN

There must be more to life than having everything.

MAURICE SENDAK

When you have only two pennies left in the world, buy a loaf of bread with one, and a lily with the other.

CHINESE PROVERB

You're only here for a short visit. Don't hurry. Don't worry. And be sure to smell the flowers along the way.

WALTER HAGEN

If we have a patient mind, all things will unfold in a natural and organic way. Patience means staying in a state of balance regardless of what is happening, staying easy and relaxed and alert.

JOSEPH GOLDSTEIN

The great secret in life…[is] not to open your letters for a fortnight. At the expiration of that period you will find that nearly all of them have answered themselves.

ARTHUR BINSTEAD

Life just is. You have to flow with it.
Give yourself to the moment. Let it happen.
JERRY BROWN

Just chill out and reproduce. Keep the species alive.
ICE-T

I have a simple philosophy.
Fill what's empty. Empty what's full.
And scratch where it itches.
ALICE ROOSEVELT LONGWORTH

Struggle mightily until you realize that you are
everything and there is no need to struggle.
DALE BORGLUM

Create the Life
You Like

Each of us is given a bit of the raw material of life with which to work. We can shape it any way we wish. The time in which we live, our inheritance of traits, etc., all have something to do with what we become, but after that it is in our hands to do much with what we have. Physically and mentally we can shape it any way we desire.

LOUIS L'AMOUR

Our lives are like an exploding sky rocket—the kind you might use in a 4th of July nighttime fireworks display. Inside the rocket are elements that burst into brilliant, cascading colors, illuminating the darkness, attracting the "oohs" and "ahs" of people. Like the rocket you have something inside you, that's there to get out, to explode.

CY EBERHART

When you discover your mission, you will feel its demand. It will fill you with enthusiasm and a burning desire to get to work on it.

W. CLEMENT STONE

When you are working toward fulfilling your true
purpose, you discover astonishing gifts within yourself
that you may have never known you have.

CHÉRIE CARTER-SCOTT

Figure out what makes you tick and go with it. If you do,
life will be blissful. If you try to go against it, the universe
will give you a swift kick in the pants.

ED BRODOW

If you do follow your bliss, you put yourself on a
kind of track that has been there all the while,
waiting for you, and the life that you ought to be living is
the one you are living.

JOSEPH CAMPBELL

You nourish your soul by fulfilling your destiny.

HAROLD S. KUSHNER

You have to take life as it happens, but you should try to
make it happen the way you want to take it.

GERMAN PROVERB

The value of life lies not in the length of days
but in the use we make of them.

MICHEL DE MONTAIGNE

The greatest use of life is to spend it for
something that will outlast it.

WILLIAM JAMES

Every man has a mandate to fill the contours of his being.

GUY DAVENPORT

Acting as if you were what you want to become and know
you can become is the way to remove self-doubt and enter
your real-magic kingdom.

WAYNE DYER

Don't wait for extraordinary opportunities. Seize
common occasions and make them great.

ORISON SWETT MARDEN

Too many of us consent, or are forced, to spend time doing things for which we have no heartfelt reason....
We do it to hold a job, to make a living, to satisfy the expectations of others, to fill our time, to evade the fact that we don't know what else to do—but not because the doing comes from inside us. When our action is dictated by factors external to our soul, we do not live active lives, but reactive lives.

PARKER J. PALMER

Your work is going to fill a large part of your life, and the only way to be truly satisfied is to do what you believe is great work. And the only way to do great work is to love what you do. If you haven't found it yet, keep looking. Don't settle.

S T E V E J O B S

Lives, like money, are spent.
What are you buying with yours?
ROY H. WILLIAMS

You can't hit a home run unless you step up to the plate.
You can't catch fish unless you put your line in the water.
You can't reach your goals if you don't try.
KATHY SELIGMAN

All the answers you are looking for are already within
your grasp: all you need to do is look inside, listen, and
trust yourself. There is no outside source of wisdom that
can give you the answers to any of your innermost
questions; you alone are your wisest teacher. Deep inside,
you already know all you need to know.
CHÉRIE CARTER-SCOTT

Two agendas are prevalent in your life: Heaven's and
yours. Often these two will clash with each other.
When what we want our lives to be is different from our
intended destiny, the universal will creates roadblocks.
CHIN-NING CHU

If we are facing in the right direction, all we have to do is keep on walking.

JACOB GOLDSTEIN

Each person on this planet is inherently, intrinsically capable of attaining "dizzying heights" of happiness and fulfillment.

WAYNE DYER

What a wonderful life
I've had! I only wish
I'd realized it sooner.

COLETTE

There is only one success—to be able to spend your life
in your own way.

CHRISTOPHER MORLEY

God asks no man whether he will accept life. That is not
the choice. One must take it. The only question is how.

HENRY WARD BEECHER

Life will have just as much meaning for you
as you put into it.

WILL DURANT

If life doesn't offer a game worth playing,
then invent a new one.

ANTHONY J. D'ANGELO

And life is what we make it.
Always has been, always will be.

GRANDMA MOSES

I've read the last page
of the Bible. It's going to turn
out all right.

BILLY GRAHAM

Index to Authors

ABOUT THE AUTHOR

Allen Klein is a bestselling author and an award-winning professional speaker. In his keynote presentations and workshops he shows people worldwide how to use humor to deal with their changes, challenges, and not-so-funny stuff. In addition to this book, Klein is also the author of *Change Your Life!: A Little Book of Big Ideas, Inspiration for a Lifetime,* and *The Art of Living Joyfully,* among others.

For more information about Klein or his presentations, go to www.allenklein.com or e-mail him at humor@allenklein.com.

To Our Readers

Viva Editions publishes books that inform, enlighten, and entertain. We do our best to bring you, the reader, quality books that celebrate life, inspire the mind, revive the spirit, and enhance lives all around. Our authors are practical visionaries: people who offer deep wisdom in a hopeful and helpful manner. Viva was launched with an attitude of growth and we want to spread our joy and offer our support and advice where we can to help you live the Viva way: vivaciously!

We're grateful for all our readers and want to keep bringing you books for inspired living. We invite you to write to us with your comments and suggestions, and what you'd like to see more of. You can also sign up for our online newsletter to learn about new titles, author events, and special offers.

Viva Editions
2246 Sixth St.
Berkeley, CA 94710
www.vivaeditions.com
(800) 780-2279
Follow us on Twitter @vivaeditions
Friend/fan us on Facebook